First English Words
Activity Book

Niki Joseph
Hans Mol

2

English puzzles and
games for children

Collins

1 London Bridge Street
London SE1 9GF

First edition 2014

Reprint 10 9 8 7 6

© HarperCollins Publishers 2014

ISBN 978-0-00-752312-2

Collins ® is a registered trademark of
HarperCollins Publishers Limited

www.collinselt.com

A catalogue record for this book is available
from the British Library

Printed and bound by Martins the Printers

Artwork by Aptara

Audio recordings by Chatterbox

Photo credits:
Photos on p44 are from Shutterstock © PhotoSky;
scubaluna; kao; Pan Xunbin; Awe Inspiring Images;
val lawless

🎧 Audio

Audio recordings of the key words from each unit of *First English Words Activity Book 2* are
available to download from **www.collinselt.com/firstenglishwords**. If you have bought this
book as part of the *First English Words Activity Pack*, you can find the audio for all components of
the pack on the CD at the back of the Teacher's Book.

The track listing for the key words in *Activity Book 2* is as follows:

Contents

Notes for parents and teachers

The *First English Words* activity books make learning English possible for very young children. They are full of activities that will encourage children to play and learn whilst having fun.

Activity Book 2 is for 4-5 year-old children. With children of this age, it is important that they enjoy learning and playing with the language. They will not remember all the words immediately, and you should not expect them to. First, they will understand the meaning of the words. Next, they will begin to slowly start saying the words. They will not begin by speaking in sentences – remember this is all about *first words*!

The tasks are slightly more difficult than those in Activity Book 1, and children are sometimes expected to practise writing words. There are many different activities in the book, such as circling, connecting the dots, counting, drawing, colouring, speaking and matching.

Features

The activity books have some important features that help children aged 4–5 when learning. Every page is clearly presented and organised.

Unit number

Activity symbols

Notes for teachers and parents

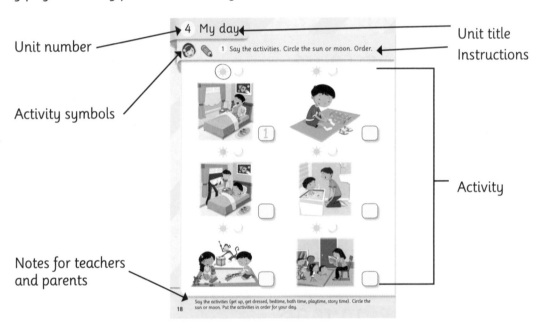

Unit title

Instructions

Activity

Activity symbols

There are six symbols that show the children what to do:

 Point

 Count out loud

 Trace, **circle**, **match** or **write**

 Say the words

 Colour parts of the picture

 Find the object

Have fun learning English with *First English Words Activity Book 2*!

This book belongs to

_____

1 Point, say and colour.

Point to the breakfast food. Say the words (milk, honey, jam, juice, cereal, bread) and colour the pictures.

1

2

Look at the pictures. Circle the differences in picture 2.

3 Trace the letters. Match.

jam   honey   spoon   tea

Look at the words and trace the letters. Then trace the lines to match each word to the correct picture.

My breakfast

Trace and colour your favourite breakfast items. Say what is on your tray.

1 Point, say and colour.

Point to the family members. Say who they are (grandpa, brother, mummy, daddy, sister, grandma). Colour the pictures.

2 Trace the letters to write the words.

 me

grandpa

 sister

grandma

 daddy

 brother

 mummy

Write the words.

3 Draw the next person.

Say the words for the people in Ben's family. Draw the next one.

12

4 Draw your family. Write their names.

Draw your family. Write their names.

123 ✏️ 1 Say, count and write.

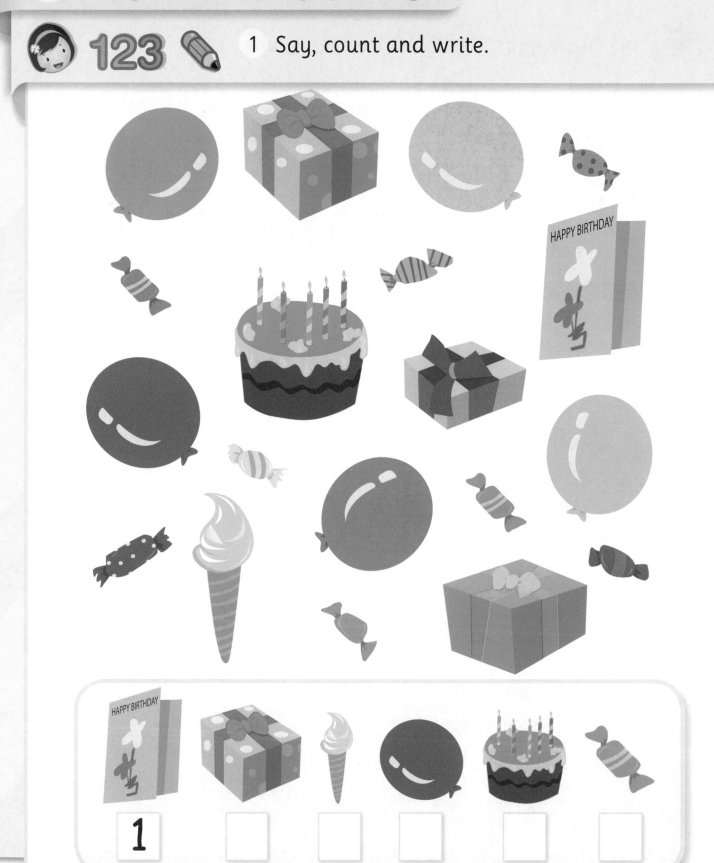

HAPPY BIRTHDAY					
1					

Say the words (birthday card, birthday present, ice-cream, balloon, birthday cake, sweet).
Count and write how many there are of each object.

2 Match, say and colour.

Match the presents to the objects and say the words. Colour your favourite present.

3 Trace the line and draw the candles.

Trace the line and draw the right number of candles. The number of candles is written on their T-shirts.

 4 Trace the words and colour the birthday card.

Happy birthday

Trace 'Happy birthday' and colour the birthday card.

4 My day

  1 Say the activities. Circle the sun or moon. Order.

Say the activities (get up, get dressed, bedtime, bath time, playtime, story time). Circle the sun or moon. Put the activities in order for your day.

2 Colour by numbers. Say the words.

Colour by numbers. Say the words (teddy bear, shoes, blocks, book, duck).

3 Circle the differences.

Circle the differences between the two pictures.

4 Write the words. Match.

bedtime

playtime

story time

bath time

Trace the words and then match them to the pictures.

5 My classroom

Match the classroom items and say the words (books, computer, chair, bag, exercise book, toy).

2 Trace the letters. Tick (✓) the items.

whiteboard
book
bag

☐   ☐   ☐

☐   ☐   ☐

Trace the words and tick the pictures they refer to.

3 Draw, colour and say.

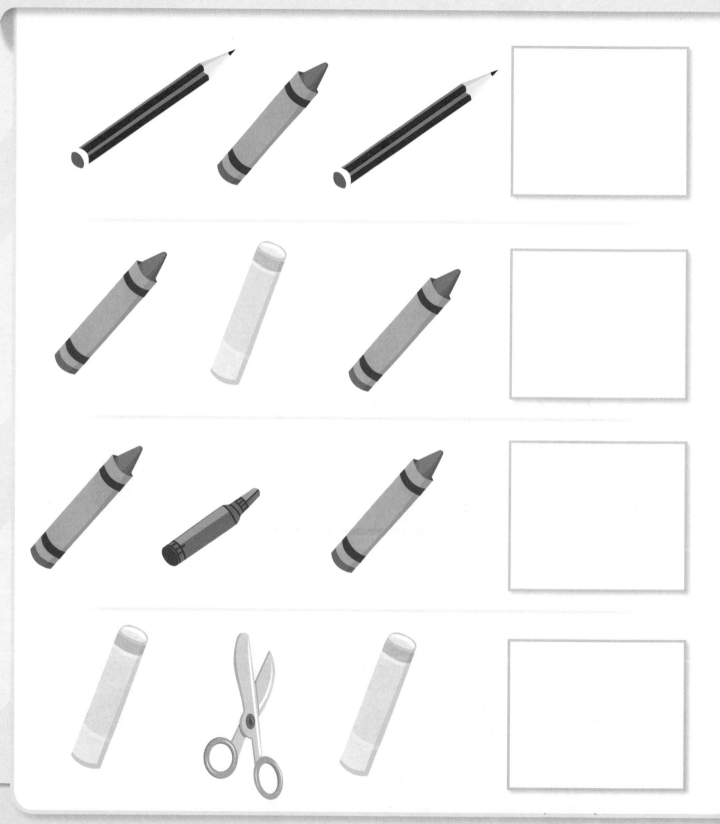

Draw the next item in the sequence. Colour the items and say the words (pencil, crayon, glue, marker, scissors).

4 Draw yourself in your classroom.

This is me in my classroom!

Draw a picture of yourself in your classroom. Colour your drawing.

6 Playtime in the park

   1 Match and say the words.

Draw a line to the objects in the main picture. Say the words (kite, football, hat, kick scooter).

2 Trace the lines and colour the hats.

Trace the lines and find out who has which kite. Colour the hats to match the kites.

3 Help Ben find the ball. Draw and colour.

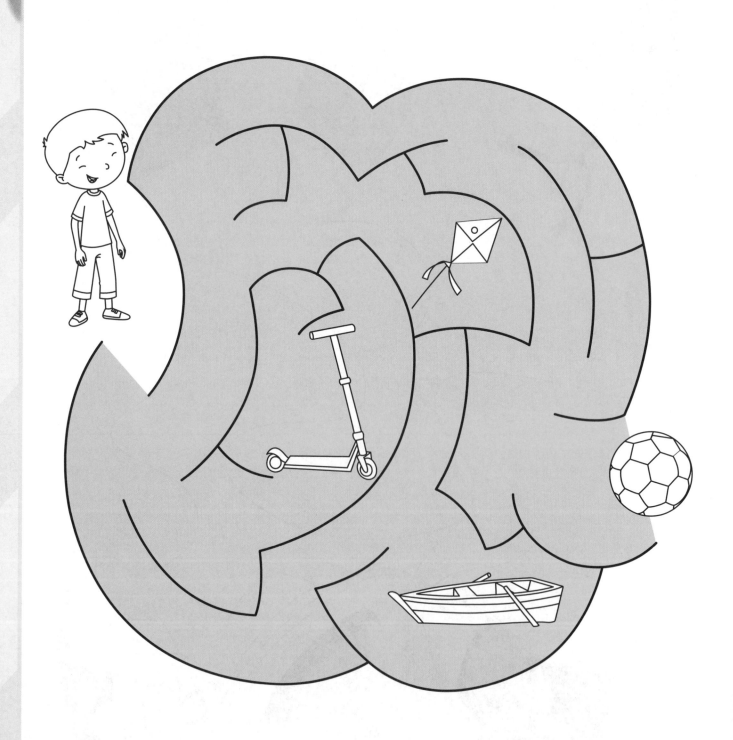

Draw a line through the maze from Ben to the ball. Colour all the items.

4 Write, say and match.

slide

ball

swing

kite

boat

scooter

Write the words. Match the words to the pictures. Say the words (kite, scooter, boat, ball, swing, slide).

7 The weather

1 Draw lines and colour.

Draw lines to where these belong. Say the weather words (rainy, cold, windy, sunny, cloudy, snowy) and colour.

1

cloudy

2

hot

Circle the differences in picture 1. Trace the words.

3 Connect the dots. Colour, write and say.

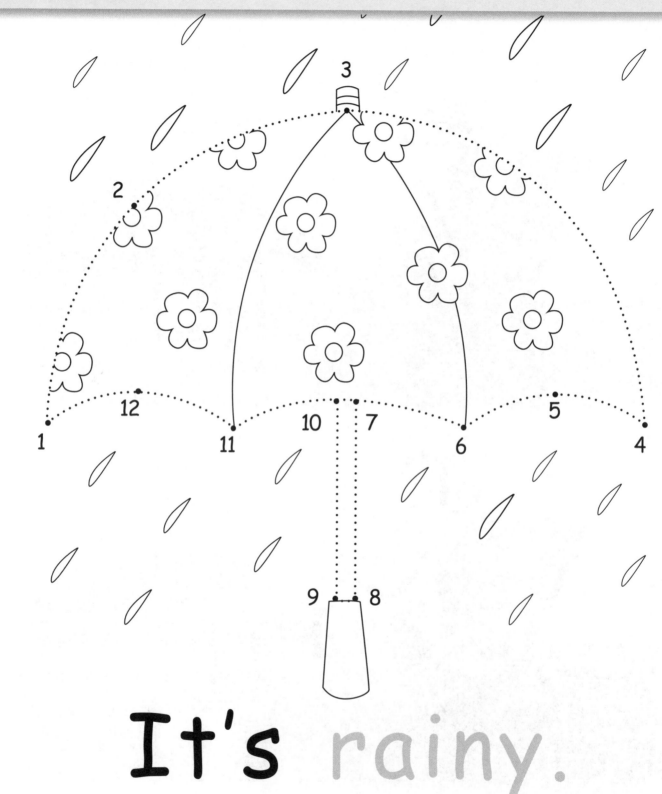

It's rainy.

Connect the dots. Colour the picture. Write the word. Say what the weather is like.

4 Draw today's weather in the window.

Draw a picture of the weather today in the window. Colour the picture.

1 Say, colour and write.

cat

puppy

hamster

rabbit

kitten

tortoise

Say the words (puppy, cat, rabbit, hamster, kitten, tortoise). Colour the animals and complete the words.

123 2 Count. Circle the groups with the same number.

Count the pets. Circle the group in each row that has the same number as the first picture.

3 Help the cat find her kitten. Say the words.

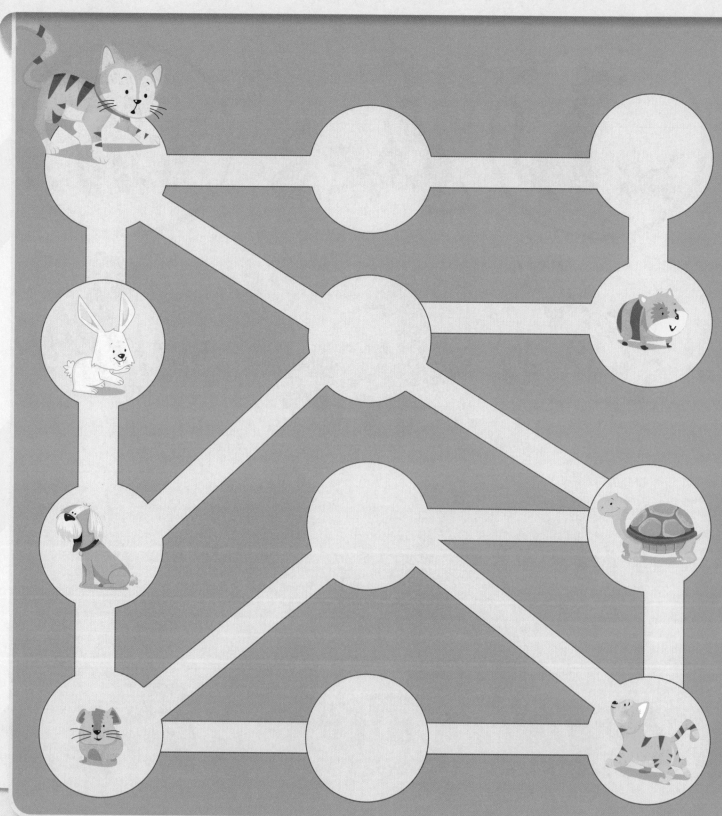

Draw a line through the maze. Say the words for the animals you find along the way
(rabbit, guinea-pig, dog, tortoise, hamster).

Draw and colour your favourite animal. Write the word.

9 On the farm

123 ✏️ 🖍️ **1** Count and write the number. Colour.

Count the animals and write the number. Colour the animals.

Match the animals to the eyes. Say the words (horse, chicken, cow, duck, donkey).

1   2   3   4   5   1   2   3   4   5

1   2   3   4   5   1   2   3   4   5

Count the sheep and circle the number. Say the number of sheep (two, five, four, three).

4 Say and write.

chicken

donkey

duck

horse

cow

sheep

Say the words (chicken, goose, donkey, duck, horse, cow, sheep). Write the words.

10 Safari sports day

1 Match and say.

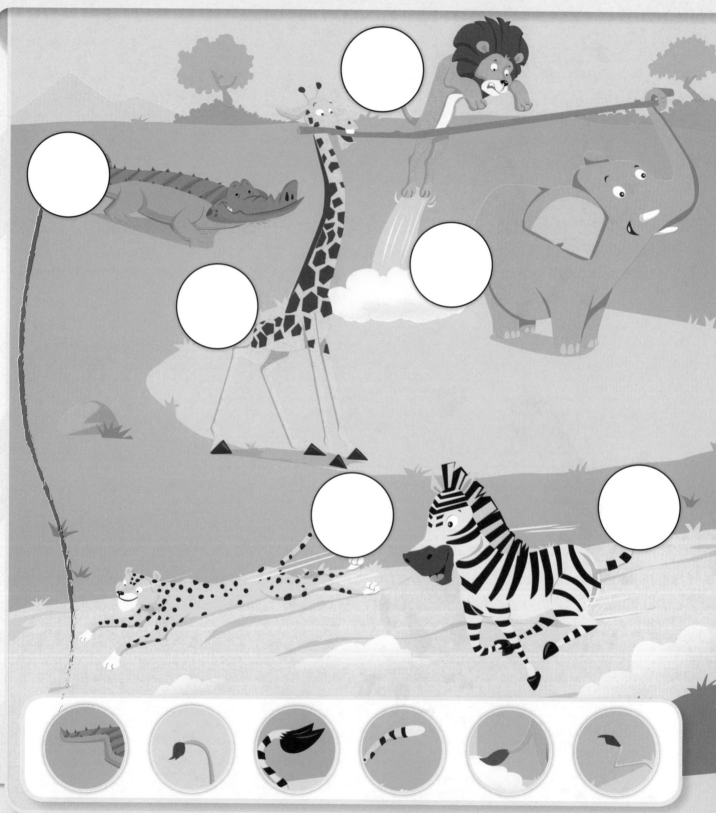

Match the tails to the animals. Say the words (crocodile, giraffe, lion, elephant, cheetah, zebra).

Look at the sequence and circle the next animal. Say the words (cheetah, zebra, crocodile, elephant, lion, giraffe).

3 Match. Say the words.

Match the skin to the animal. Say the words (crocodile, elephant, lion, giraffe, cheetah, zebra).

44

4 Draw and colour your favourite safari animal.

Draw and colour your favourite safari animal. Say its name.

11 Jungle animals

  1 Where are the animals? Match and say.

Draw lines to the animals in the picture. Say the words (monkey, tiger, parrot, snake, iguana, leopard).

2 Colour and say.

Colour. Say the name of the animal and the colours.

3 Count. Colour the bowls with three snakes.

Count the snakes. Colour the bowls with three snakes.

4 Draw a path and say.

Go from start to finish. Draw your path and say the words (monkey, tiger, parrot, snake, iguana, leopard).

12 In the rock pool

   1 Draw, say and colour.

Trace over the lines and colour. Say the words for the animals (starfish, jellyfish, seahorse, crab, shell, fish).

 **2** Circle the next animal. Say the name of the animal.

Circle the next sea animal in the sequence. Say the words (shell, starfish, seahorse, crab, fish, jellyfish).

3 Circle the differences.

1

2

Circle the differences between the aquariums.

 **4** Draw your favourite sea animals. Colour.

Draw favourite sea animals in the aquarium and colour.

13 My town

1 Trace Ben's route.

Trace the boy's route. Say the names of the places he cycles past (swimming pool, school, library, toy shop, supermarket).

54

2 Match the items to the places. Say the words.

Draw lines between items and places. Say the words (bag/school, swimming costume/
swimming pool, book/library, apple/supermarket, rocket/toy shop).

55

3 Colour the things you see in a library. Say.

Colour the things you find in a library. Say the words (book, bookcase, computer, chair, table).

4 This is your new bike. Colour it!

Colour the bike in your favourite colours.

14 Clothes

123   **1** Count, write the numbers and say the words.

Count all the clothes of the same type and write numbers. Say the words (t-shirt, scarf, hat, skirt, trousers, shorts). The clothes can be different from the pictures in the box.

2 Write and match.

shorts

scarf

hat

skirt

trousers

t-shirt

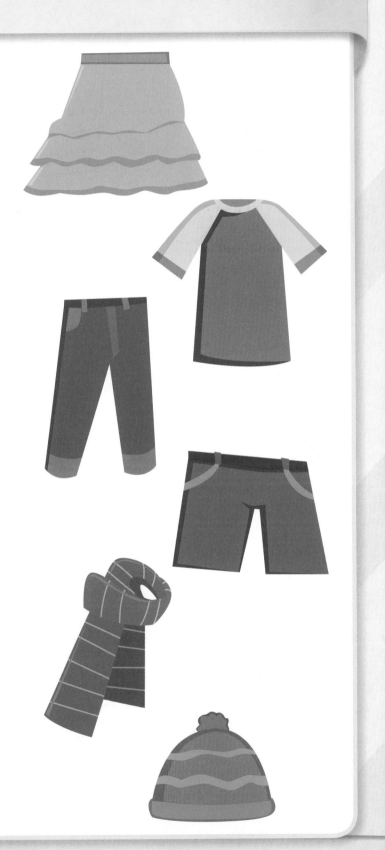

Write the words. Match the words to the pictures.

3 Colour and match.

Colour the clothes you wear in winter blue, and the clothes you wear in summer red.

 **4** Draw yourself wearing your favourite clothes.

Draw yourself wearing your favourite clothes. Say the words (shorts, scarf, hat, skirt, trousers, t-shirt) and colour them.

Say the words!

Goodbye

Are you good at English? Colour one, two or three stars. Do you like the activities in this book? Colour one of the faces.